* Independent of your e-book trailer status (whether you have one playing on your site or you are still in the process of creating one), you can get started right away in the planning and preparation of your marketing strategy.

I0472928

Step 1 – GET STARTED

Why You Need to Market and Promote Your Book With a Book Trailer

First, what is a book trailer? A trailer is a short video (usually 1 to 3 minutes in length) that serves to inform your readers about your book, about you as the author, and/or about a topic related to the book. Therefore, because it can "hit on" a broad spectrum of information, the book trailer can be an extremely effective media strategy to market your book.

However, book trailers ALONE will not make your book a bestseller!

Book trailers should make up just one part of a well-thought-out marketing strategy. Also, as with any marketing tool, book trailers need to have a purpose and should be created very intentionally. As you will see in the following pages, there are many types of trailers – and even more ways to use them – to generate book sales and to create a base of dedicated readers.

One of the particular benefits of book trailers is that they are highly PORTABLE. This makes them quite a useful tool in the electronic age. Once you produce your book trailer, with its creatively embedded marketing message, you can do the following:

1. *Post it to your YouTube channel* – a free service that happens to be the second largest search engine next to Google. Add the right search tags, and your book trailer – thus your book – can be found potentially by anyone and everyone.

How to Market Your Book With a Book Trailer Is for You If:

- You are an author – self-published or with a publisher – who wants a creative way to promote your book.
- You need a resource that will give you insider tips for online promotions and time-proven methods to build an online community of fans.
- You are ready to create a more competitive profile of your book in order to attract more readers.
- You want senior level professionals in the book marketing and publishing field to share with you a more comprehensive marketing plan to engage your audience.
- You seek to expand your readership and SELL BOOKS.

An Easy-to-Implement 5-Step Process

We have divided the book into 5 steps: 1) Get Started, 2) Plan a Successful Outcome, 3) Determine Your Readiness, 4) Get It Done, and 5) Take the Next Steps. We will lead you through each step with the latest information we can find about all the best practices in marketing: what they are and when, where, how, and why they work.

Then, in each section, we will suggest you take on certain mini-projects. These projects will allow you to duplicate the efforts of the successful authors and marketers you will learn about and will encourage you to follow some tested marketing principles.

These mini-projects have skill divisions associated with them to help you best schedule your time and your efforts to get the overall project – your book trailer – created and implemented. These skill division categories will also help you determine your expectations, your abilities and your potential limitations. First, you will examine what you expect the trailer to do for the marketing of your book. In other words, is it feasible, or are you actually thinking too little of its potential? You will also examine whether or not you are able to complete the project yourself or whether you need assistance. In each case, you will also examine time and finally learn part of the meaning behind the axiom "Time will tell."

A Note From the Authors

As authors and professionals in fields related to publishing, we have written this e-book to help you create an exciting marketing plan for your book – through the development and promotion of a book trailer. As we work with you through the process, we will:

- Share the 5 easy-to-follow steps that will take you from little or no online promotion to wide online exposure.
- Share ideas that will attract your readers' attention.
- Suggest good marketing messages, some of which will depend on your book's genre.
- Assist you in an evaluation of how ready you are to follow up on your best-fit promotion plan.
- Suggest additional helpful resources to enhance your learning process as you head toward marketing success.

Using our time-proven marketing strategies, we will guide you through each of the 5 Steps. One of our priorities will be to help you create unique online marketing strategies that will be as distinctive as you are as an author.

* Whether you already have a book trailer, are in the process of putting one together or have just started to consider the possibilities of a book trailer – this e-book is for you!

2. *Post it to Facebook* – the site that Americans spend more time on than any other Internet site. Studies show that 500 million users, on average, spend more than 55 minutes per day on Facebook (Digital Buzz, Facts & Figures 2010). According to the 2010 PEW Internet American Online Research study, 28% of those users post about their buying experiences, a fact that could definitely have an impact on your book sales.

3. *Add it to your personal Web site and blog.* Studies show that 58% of shoppers report searching online before they shop and 52% report shopping online (2010 PEW Internet American Online Research). Therefore, one way to capture their interest and to sell your book is to make sure your book trailer finds its way to them via your Web site or your blog.

4. *Insert it as a link in articles and reports.* This sort of strategic placement of a book trailer can further enhance your credibility as an author as it also gains exposure for your book.

When should you start to plan your book trailer? Many authors, even before they begin to write, have begun to "create a vision" for the plot and have settled on the purpose of their books. As a result, they can, quite early in the process, choose ideas or images to include in their book trailers – ideas to best highlight their points and images to connect with their readers. For novice writers, however, it may be more helpful to write the whole book before giving consideration to the book trailer. In some substantial way the writing process may help them gain the insight they need about what to include in a trailer. Also, novice authors most likely will not comprehend what is involved with marketing until they try to sell a finished book. However, an already successful author probably has the experience – or a new author working with an editor, marketing professional and social media assistant can be guided – to write the book and to plan for its marketing simultaneously. Therefore, the timing of the steps in this plan will vary from author to author. What will not change is the importance the book trailer can have in the success of an author's book promotion strategy.

In today's competitive marketplace, where reader attention is at a premium, you will be sure to experience a return on your investment with a video marketing plan that includes your book trailer. Not only will you get the word out and drive more sales, but you also will showcase your book through the use of images, one of the most effective strategies to influence buyers.

Step 2 – Plan a Successful Outcome

Planning upfront to finish well will save you time and ensure you do not duplicate your efforts. If you create a vision of what your best-case outcome looks like, that vision will ensure you stay on track. As you complete the various steps, you can measure each step against your desired outcome as you progress toward the successful completion and implementation of your book trailer.

How to Plan Your Successful Book Trailer Marketing Strategy

Your genre, the topic of your book, and the marketing purpose of the book trailer all work together to determine what the format and content of the book trailer will be, how the trailer should be produced and how and where the trailer will be promoted.

You, as the author, should also determine what your actual marketing needs are. For example, you may need the book trailer to help you do any or all of the following:

1. Generate interest in the book's upcoming release
2. Introduce one of the book's characters
3. Update readers on a character in a book series
4. Introduce the story behind the author's topic
5. Develop interest in a sequel
6. Create interest in an issue the book addresses
7. Promote an event around the book's theme
8. Provoke discussion about a hot topic
9. Educate and inform readers about any aspect of the book
10. Introduce yourself to your readers
11. Present yourself as a subject matter expert

* Note: From our experience as authors and as professionals working with authors, we can assure you that some aspects of your branding (for example, finding ways either to engage your readers or to promote yourself as an author) will require more effort on your part than others. This is especially true if you are new to publishing, and you may find it best to work with your co-authors and/or editors or publisher to devise a marketing plan. In this case, it also will be more time effective to consider the marketing plans for your book trailer at an early stage. Not only will you then have the book trailer campaign ready at the appropriate time, you will be able to incorporate it into the plan you have scheduled for all the other marketing events surrounding the launch of the actual book. However, if you are a novice writer, where the task of writing itself can be overwhelming – and you are not yet working with an experienced editor and marketing professional – you may need to consider working sequentially through the process: 1) Do research, 2) outline book, 3) write book, 4) plan marketing strategy, 5) create book trailer, and 6) implement marketing strategy. Just know that when you choose not to multitask, the process is slower,

but it can still be effective.

To get an idea of the types of book trailers that are successful in your field and genre, perform some online research. Ways to do that include the following:

1. Visit various search engines (Google, Yahoo, etc.) and type in the keywords of your genre and add "+ book trailers" [Example: historical fiction + book trailers].

2. Study the genre's successful authors and benchmark yourself to them.
- Visit their Web sites and other online sites to find certain answers. Which of their online sites are most visited? Which have the most comments and/or other audience interaction?
- Go to YouTube to see which trailers get the most hits.
- View the Facebook fan pages of your favorite authors to see what they are doing with their book trailers.

Once you have identified some successful authors, follow their marketing strategies full circle. Visit their Web sites and note how they promote their books. Do they have blogs? If so, read several posts. Do the authors have links to their social media sites? If so, visit each type of site (YouTube, Twitter, Facebook and Google+) to see what you can find. If they do not have social media buttons on their site, use search engines to find profiles and other information about the author – some of which is readily available in book reviews and press releases. (Note: Links on your Web site to connect readers to your other social media sites are important marketing tools.)

When you do such a full-circle examination of the ways your favorite authors promote their books, you will gain many insights into what you, too, can do. You will, no doubt, find at least one idea you can adapt and then add to the techniques you use to create and to market your own book trailer.

Because new book trailers are being uploaded daily it is worthwhile to do frequent searches while you plan your book trailer. Frequent searches will also keep you updated on all the potential styles and formats, which change quite often with the adaptation of new technologies.

During the process of planning for a successful outcome, we suggest that you become familiar with the options available for producing a book trailer. In so doing, you will make sure that you have provided the production time needed in order to have the book trailer ready and available at the time your book and its marketing campaign are launched.

Book trailers can be do-it-yourself (DIY) projects or professionally produced videos. In other words, you can produce them on your computer with the software that comes loaded with your PC or Mac, or you can hire a videographer who uses a full-production studio. How you choose to produce your book trailer will depend on the purpose of your trailer, on the niche you want to penetrate, on the resources available to you, and on the professionalism and standards expected in the medium you wish to use. You can produce very effective trailers with a variety of resources. Reference our Resources section at the end of this e-book for suggestions.

What You Can Do to Duplicate Good Results: Assessment and Evaluation

Ask yourself two basic questions. What can YOU do? What should you outsource? Consider the following to help you decide:

Am I willing to:
1. Research best practices to develop a marketing plan?

a. Learn what is working for successful authors in my genre?
b. Analyze what media platforms get the most readers' attention?
2. Write content for my book trailer and promotion?
   a. Learn what really gets people interested in reading books in my genre and incorporate that into the promotional material for my book?
   b. Write content that grabs and keeps attention?
3. Learn the outlets to promote my book trailer?
   a. Learn more about social media?
   b. Learn to speak professionally?
   c. Create an online following?
   d. Search out and use both online and offline resources to generate a buzz?
4. Spend time away from writing to promote?
   a. Develop an interest in book promotion?
   b. Spend the time necessary to promote?

If you say no to more than 2 or 3 of the above, you would do well to work with a social media assistant and marketing branding professional. A professional's initial assessment, usually free, will give you the insight to evaluate the skills you already have and the skills or resources you need to acquire. In addition, it will give you a range of available options to choose from in order to complete the book trailer project in a way that will serve you and be appropriate for your target audience.

Insider Professional Tips

As long-time service providers to writers and authors, we would like to take the time to share with you some of our best tips and practices so that you can benefit from our past experience and save yourself precious time. You may even sidestep a few frustrating moments!

Some of our favorite tips relating to this topic:

* Follow a successful author in your genre. Determine what works. Duplicate what works. You will notice most book trailers are no more than 3 minutes. (One to 3 minutes is considered the optimal length.)

* Use online schedulers like Hootesuite and Socialoomph to automate the posting of your promotional messages to social media platforms such as Facebook, LinkedIn, Twitter and YouTube.

A Word of Caution: While online schedulers are great for creating a campaign for a certain purpose, the most read, followed, and clicked-on forms of social interaction are those made LIVE in PERSON by YOU. So, while these tools are helpful, make sure you also spend time interacting with your fans as often as possible on each of your social media sites.

* Develop text templates. You can then easily cut and paste promotional text into various online platforms to promote your video. Just make sure you edit appropriately after the cut and paste, as well as add, whenever possible, original content to suit that particular platform.

Measure Your Success

Each social media platform has unique measurement tools to track such things as site visits and numbers of clicks. These tools will provide you with online help menus and tutorials to explain the reports and the significance of the measures they track. For example, Twitter has a Twitter Grader, Web sites have Google Analytics and blogging platforms have their own metric reporting tools.

If you load your trailer on YouTube or any other video sharing site, you will at least be able to measure the number of hits/views on your trailer. Additionally, you will be able to gauge the interest of your readers by noting how many subscribe to your YouTube video channel.

Other platforms allow you to track the number of times your trailer gets shared. Statistics in these platforms will give you access to details such as the number of times your trailer is shared by other bloggers or inserted in articles by other writers or reviewers.

Caveats and Concluding Thoughts

Marketing your book trailer takes a lot of time since you must first write your promotional content to suit online media. Then, for the material to be most effective, you must have the knowledge of how online conversations are conducted, how search engines drive traffic to your book trailer and how to publish content that inspires others to share. Once you have a sense of all these factors, you can schedule it appropriately on the various online media.

Since online communities have various informational tools that allow you to track the online activity of your audience, you need to be dedicated to noting the daily changes that occur online and among the members of your audience. Such tools will help you determine how your marketing messages are being received so that you can reach out in a proactive manner to keep your presence as an author current and relevant. Because this e-book helps you to plan for a communication campaign highlighted by a video product – your book trailer – you should consider the following statistics as relevant ones to monitor: 1) the number of views your video gets, 2) the number of times it is shared, 3) the number of times it is included in someone else's playlist of favorites, 4) the number of times the link is shared and 5) the number of times the video is embedded in other online content.

Resource Check: If the tracking and analyses of such data are time commitments in which you are unwilling to invest, consider working with professionals who can perform these functions on your behalf.

Step 3 - DETERMINE YOUR READINESS

Am I Ready and Willing?

To market your book trailer you will need to:

1. Know your audience and know where you can find them online.
2. Inform yourself about the various software tools used for online promotion.
3. Create your story arc. Just like your book, the trailer should have a beginning, middle and end. You can format your book trailer in a variety of ways; popular formats include short interviews, a series of testimonials, or a mix of words and phrases set to music. Whatever format you use, make sure you have carefully prepared the "story" of the trailer.
4. Be honest with yourself about your technical skills and challenges.

Resource Check: You may need the help of a marketing professional and social media assistant if you are not willing and ready.

Am I Able and Capable?

To successfully market your book trailer you will need to:
1. Devote time and energy to writing content.
2. Spend time posting online.
3. Spend time engaging with your reader.

Resource Check: You may need the help of marketing professional, an experienced editor, and social media assistant if you are not able and capable.

Brand Readiness

A book trailer can be a successful component of your marketing strategy whether you are a first-time author or an established author.

The book trailer can help you do all the following and more:

1. Generate interest in the book's upcoming release
2. Introduce one of the book's characters
3. Update readers on a character in a book series
4. Introduce the story behind the author's topic
5. Develop interest in a sequel
6. Create interest in an issue the book addresses
7. Promote an event around the book's theme
8. Provoke discussion about a hot topic
9. Educate and inform readers about any aspect of the book
10. Introduce yourself to your readers
11. Present yourself as a subject matter expert

* Note: In Step 2, How to Plan Your Successful Book Trailer Marketing Strategy, you began to consider which of the above 11 goals are currently the most relevant to you as an author. During that step you began to choose and design the events that would allow you to roll out your book trailer marketing campaign in a manner that would both meet your goals and, ultimately, engage more of your audience. During this step, we ask that you take ACTION on your decisions.

*Resource Check: If you are having a tough time honing in on your goals or your plan, ask for input from your respected colleagues or your publisher, or seek the assistance of a branding and marketing professional.

Commitment and Suggested Schedule

Although the initial time investment to set up a book trailer on social media platforms is lengthy, once that is accomplished you are able to add content or to respond to your readers quickly. For example, if you are mobile savvy, you can even respond to comments via your mobile phone. An important thing to remember is that daily online interaction and correspondence with your readers is critical and will keep interest in you and your book at a high level.

Plan your promotion strategies around special events that promote your book: the all-important book release, book readings, reviews, etc. The timing, of course, will depend on the type of event. Just before and just after the release of the book, for example, you may want to do daily promotions. Later, weekly efforts may be enough to maintain interest.

Step 4 – GET IT DONE

Tools and Materials

To promote your book trailer online you will need to open accounts in the following. If you already have established accounts, all the better. You can begin to market as soon as your book trailer is created.

1. Facebook Fan Page
2. Blog
3. Web Site
4. Twitter
5. Topic-specific Online Sites (writing, genre, author, etc.)

Task Description: Where to Submit the Trailer

Now the FUN begins. You can do so many things to build a marketing campaign that integrates your trailer with other online tools. Try some (or all) of the following:

1. Tweet, tweet, and retweet. Link your followers to your video and ask for feedback.
2. Use Facebook to "share" the video link and ask for feedback and comments.
3. Add the video to your Facebook fan page.
4. Add the book trailer to the side bar of your blog or Web site.
5. Make sure your Web site has a Google+ button and ask your friends to + the page where you have embedded the video.
6. Upload the book trailer to Amazon, Barnes & Noble, and any other bookseller sites you can. Then use the "share" button to send out the link.
7. Upload your video to YouTube and Vimeo and use the social sharing buttons to spread the link out over the Web.
8. Strategically partner with other authors and subject matter experts. Interview each other, ask each other to be guest

bloggers, promote each other and share your video.

9. Put the titles of your books on your business cards, in your e-mail signature, and on any other print materials you use in marketing. Also include a link to the video.

10. Capture names and e-mail addresses of people who visit your Web site or blog. Send them the video link as well as other updates about your books and book signings.

11. Interview other authors and get interviewed by them. Share your video, along with all the other information about your book, at every possible opportunity. Fellow authors may give you a spot on their blogs and Web sites, especially if you reciprocate.

No matter how you build your marketing strategy, make sure you ALWAYS write or call (if possible) to personally thank those who interview you, comment, tweet, "like", +, and BUY your book. When you do that, you build loyalty. And those loyal fans will quickly become your champions!

Tips and Best Practices

If you are already a known author, you can use a book trailer to do the following:

1. *Serve as online "bonus" material.* Web sites for television shows (as well as movie DVDs) often provide bonus materials that expand on details about the actors or the story. Fans love the opportunity to gain such inside information. Book trailers and blogs can be a great way to do the same for your readers, as well as to provide "scoops" in the form of a "Story to be continued…" blurb between two books in a series or as a news story about how your book has influenced some reader.
2. *Promote other services and products.* Cross-promotion efforts can expand both your business influence and your book sales, when you mention your other services in your book and vice versa.
3. *Establish yourself as a subject matter expert.* In almost every case, when others learn about your book, you will be invited

to give an opinion, give an interview or give a presentation.

4. *Send out a CALL TO ACTION.* Always end your trailers with suggestions such as "Buy this book" or "Go to my blog." After all, you want to create CUSTOMERS, so you need to tell your readers what you want them to DO.

Here are some best practices for the creation of content, both for your book trailer and for the marketing content you need to generate in order to promote and to introduce your book and book trailer:

1. **Connect with your audience's emotions.** Use short phrases and images that evoke an emotional response. Choose music that matches the mood of your book. If it's a thriller, choose music that evokes suspense. For a romance novel, choose something soulful. When you set out with the intention to speak directly to your audience on an emotional level, that emotion will serve as an effective guide to help you develop your trailer.

2. **Engage with your audience on relevant interests.** Did you know that there are online reading circles, usually devoted to certain novels, whose members swap recipes based on books they have read? If that is your audience, include your favorite recipe for, say, fudge brownies in your promotional material. If you are writing for sports fans, include a reference to a scene that has the main characters at a sports bar or in an arena.

3. **Solve a problem.** Bring in statistics to show how your book provides some sort of solution. Even fictional book trailers can use this approach. If your book is humorous, for example, cite the data about how many people are bored on Friday nights. Then, present your book as something fun that can break that Friday night monotony.

Task Description: Start Promoting Your Book Trailer and Book

Think about your target audience and how you can best reach the particular members of that audience. If you already have a following, take time to write down what you know about your readers. If you are a new author, make a list of the type of readers who might be interested in your topic.

Now that you have a list of prospects, do a little online research. If you know you will use social media, look for groups and fan pages that promote the topics and interests associated with the types of readers on your list. Then begin to post information to these sites, information that will provide something of value to each community. Always give a link back to the "landing page" that hosts your video. This offers two benefits: 1) You are able to share your knowledge of the topic with each group, and 2) the link attracts followers and fans to your online site.

Gather information about all of your personal and business contacts in one system – systems like MailChimp or Constant Contact offer various services and price points, which make them good choices for either new authors or established authors with a large following. Prior to subscribing your friends, send them an e-mail message to explain your new publishing project and to tell them you would appreciate their help in getting the word out about the project. Such sincere and heartfelt pleas for help are always much better than a heavy-handed sales attempt. Then, begin to send out informational letters about your book. Include details about the topic or plot of the book, what people will gain from reading it, where they can order it, and when it will be published. Ask your readers to spread the word. As other people begin to write to you with book inquiries, add them to your mailing list.

With each of your letters, give your readers content that helps them in some way, solves a problem for them, or explains the benefits of reading your book. This type of content will increase the chances they will make a positive buying decision.

Step 5 - TAKE THE NEXT STEPS

Before you call your book trailer a finished product and post it all over the Internet, get a second opinion. And a third. And a fourth…. Have several people who fit your intended reader profile, and who have not read your book, watch the trailer. Ask them what they think your book is about. Ask them what they would pay to buy it. This kind of feedback will help you know if your trailer truly speaks to the intended audience and if it communicates the value your audience needs.

Success Factors: Measure and Adjust

In Step 2, in the sections Measure Your Success and Caveats and Concluding Thoughts, you received an introduction to the fact that each social media platform has unique measurement tools that can track such performance measurements as site visits and numbers of clicks. You also learned how each analytic can help you determine how your marketing messages are being received.

With that in mind, begin to gauge the effectiveness of your strategy by asking some of the following questions. Are you attracting enough people (hits)? If people are reading, clicking, liking, and commenting, are they also taking the next logical step and buying (or adding their names to a mailing list)? If not, where might there be a breakdown? Does the "landing page" of your site communicate enough value to your audience? Are you sharing too much irrelevant information? Is your call to action unclear?

Having a successful marketing strategy includes tweaking along the way. In order to build a strong and consistent brand presence, you must continually test its delivery.

Success Factors: Read and Respond to Your Reader

Many people believe that social media is more disconnected than in-person interaction, but it can actually be more powerful. In fact, some feel much more comfortable and at ease with their online peers, and, as a result, are more likely to go to them for help and advice when they have a problem. That means that establishing yourself as an online expert can be quite beneficial. To do so requires you to "pipe up": to voice your opinion, to share relevant information, and to engage your audience.

Many people make a fatal business mistake with social media. They use it only to put out content and neglect its vast marketing potential, which is one of the most important opportunities it provides. Interacting with your contacts can generate a gold mine of opportunity. One of the means to extract this golden treasure requires you to spend a few minutes (ideally on a daily basis) to authentically and openly comment on the posts of others. Even simple things, such as wishing your connections a "Happy Birthday" or sending them get-well wishes when they are ill, allows you to develop a friendship that goes beyond a business relationship. In so doing, you will develop fans who will openly promote you and help you "spread the word" about your book projects. As they help you champion your cause, your success will multiply!

When you find these champions, remember to send personal thank-yous for their efforts in order to let them know just how much they mean to you.

Take a few minutes now and jot down a marketing plan for your book trailer.

Include details about your intended audience, your book's message in a nutshell, your unique perspective on the book's topic, and any other resources about your book that might help.

Ask yourself a series of questions: What online resources will you use to publish the trailer? What other media will you use to get the word out about the trailer? Who on your contact list will help you spread the word about your new book?

Where do members of your intended audience hang out? Are they into current events? Are they gardeners? Are they health and medical professionals? Make a list of as many "places" as you can possibly imagine where they might gather online.

How often will you contact your audience? Will you "tweet" twice a day? Post on Facebook once a week? Blog monthly? Send a newsletter monthly? The more frequent your contacts the better, but make sure you create a schedule that you can stick to no matter what the plan. Remember that a consistent marketing plan will help establish trust and credibility with your audience and will lead to more sales in the long run.

Create alerts in Google (google.com/alerts) so that you can receive news stories on "hot topics" that your readers will care about. Then, use your list of "hangouts" above to share these stories on your social media sites, or use the data as a basis to write your own blog posts or newsletter articles. Remember, when possible, to tie in the information to the reasons you wrote your book or to the ways your book answers the problems in the articles. Also, always provide a link to your book trailer, an opt-in page, or the sales page for your book.

Learn From a Fellow Author

In the following section, one of your fellow authors shares her most successful book trailer marketing plans, strategies and best practices in the hope that you can benefit from her lessons learned!

Once you have completed the 5 easy steps in this process and created your book trailer, you, too, have an opportunity to be featured here in our next edition! So, please send us your lessons learned (with proper attribution, as necessary).

Lessons Learned: Get More Hits

Author Gina Maddox

http://www.ginamaddox.com/

(speaksandwrites YouTube)

Author Gina Maddox has, to date, produced 4 book trailers. Since her book, *The Working Woman's Rant & Rave Guidebook,* is about a work-related topic, she has found that work-related topics for her book trailers help to guarantee she receives more hits and gains followers. They also help to increase the odds her work is picked up by bloggers and other social media.

In Her Own Words:

"After the initial release of my book and the first book trailer, I needed to do something else to jolt interest in the book. I realized that National Bosses' Day was coming up, so I used quotes about bosses from my book, and some fun statistics that I discovered from online publications, to create a special "Bosses' Day" video. Bosses' Day is a popular topic for bloggers and writers, and I was pleased to discover that a few of them linked or embedded my video in their articles. My book cover was featured in several places in my Bosses' Day video, and I spotlighted the book and my Web site at the end of the video. I actually had more hits on the Bosses' Day video than on my original book trailer. Valuable lesson learned: Make your trailer 'newsworthy' to drive viewers to it."

Gina Covell Maddox is the author of *The Working Woman's Rant & Rave Guidebook* and is at work on a new book, title to be released soon. Stay tuned to her Web site (www.ginamaddox.com) for updated information.

Remember, we would like to feature you for the next edition! So, please send in your lessons learned with proper attribution.

Encouragement

Keep at it!!! Test different ways to introduce your book trailer. Test approaches from informative to funny. Test various images and soundtracks. Above all things, be distinctly creative.

Remember that using video is particularly effective if your target audience is women. According to the Nielsen report (Social Media Report: Q3 2011), women watch more videos and men watch longer videos. Even if your target market includes both men and women, marketing with book trailers is a winning strategy. According to comScore Video Metrics, video views on the Internet surpassed 30 billion in November of 2011. On YouTube alone, the popular video sharing platform, 128.1 million viewers watched more than 12 billion videos, an average of about 94.3 videos per viewer per month.

So keep at it and, if you need a little extra help, go to the resources below.

 **RESOURCES**

Helpful resources to complement this project and to meet marketing needs for authors

- Online resources –
    - Social media: Twitter, Facebook, Linkedlin, YouTube, Vimeo, Flickr, Google.com/plus
    - Research: Google.com/alerts
    - Mailing list providers: iContact, Constant Contact, MailChimp (free)
    - Website and blog platforms: WordPress, TypePad, Tumblr
    - Plugins/add ins: RSS Graffiti (Facebook plugin); AddThis (WordPress/website plugin)
    - Statistics/analysis: AddThis, Google.com/analytics, Facebook stats, HootSuite dashboard,

- o Online schedulers: HootSuite for online social media, TweetDeck, WordPress scheduling feature
- For other marketing ideas, visit our home page at www.koreaccess.com.
- For an example of a trailer created by co-author Maggie Ruch, marketing and social media assistant, visit the following link: http://animoto.com/play/0wEpWXCRqQ EyC4SlCyJOSA

* To add your favorite helpful resource, send an e-mail to one of the co-authors. (See below for contact information.)

About the Authors

<u>Branding Communication Services</u>
You have written your book and now you are ready to generate online buzz. Allow Maria to advise and assist in crafting the online story that will have readers ready to connect with you, your plot and characters.

Free Offer: Complementary one-on-one phone consultation to discuss your sales and marketing goals and to discuss your service options.

Maria Pinochet
Communications Writer & Consultant
Kore Access, Incorporated

<u>maria@koreaccess.com</u>

www.koreaccess.com

Editing Services

You've created the story. Now your editor can make it shine. Linda is an editor who plays tough with your words so your critics can't.

Free Offer: Provide Linda with two typed pages of your writing project, and she will give you a sample of what the editing process can do for you.

Linda Wasserman
Publisher & Editor
Pelican Press Pensacola

pelicanpost@cox.net

www.pelicanpresspensacola.com

Virtual Assistant Services

Learn how Maggie at Advanced Virtual Assistant Services can help you market and promote your book. The result will be more customer attraction, a better brand presence, and better online relationship building.

Free Offer: A 30-minute review of your current social media presence will help you reach your book marketing goals.

Maggie Ruch
Advanced Virtual Assistant Services

maggie@virtualwebsiteassistant.com

virtualwebsiteasssistant.com

Input and Testimonials

We welcome and encourage your feedback.
How can we make this better?

Also, share your lessons learned for a chance to
be quoted in our next edition.

www.ingramcontent.com/pod-product-compliance
Lightning Source LLC
Chambersburg PA
CBHW071646170526
45166CB00003B/1458